meets the
**monkey**

# the :01 One minute manager meets the monkey

## meets the monkey

KEN BLANCHARD
WILLIAM ONCKEN, JR.
HAL BURROWS

HarperCollins*Publishers*

HarperCollins*Publishers*
77–85 Fulham Palace Road
Hammersmith, London, W6 8JB
www.harpercollins.co.uk

The paperback edition published 2004

24

First published in the UK by Fontana 1990

ISBN-13   978-0-00-711698-0
ISBN-10   0-00-711698-5

Set in New Caledonia

Printed and bound by
Clays Ltd, St Ives plc

# The Symbols

The One Minute Manager's symbol—a one-minute readout from the face of a modern digital watch—is intended to remind each of us to take a minute out of our day to look into the faces of the people we manage. And to realize that they are our most important resources.

The Monkey Manager's symbol—a harried manager overwhelmed by a deskful of problems—is intended to remind us to constantly discipline ourselves to invest our time on the most vital aspects of management rather than dilute our effectiveness by "doing more efficiently those things that shouldn't be done in the first place."

# INTRODUCTION

Over a decade ago a real joy came into my life—Bill Oncken. I first came into contact with Bill and his monkey-on-the-back analogy when I was given a copy of his classic November 1974 *Harvard Business Review* article entitled "Managing Management Time: Who's Got the Monkey?" that he co-authored with Donald Wass. I read it and light bulbs began to flash. At the time, I was a tenured full professor in the School of Education at the University of Massachusetts. As such, according to Bill, I was a typical northeastern intellectual bleeding-heart social theorist who thought my role in life was to wipe out pain and suffering by helping everyone. In other words, I was a compulsive monkey-picker-upper.

Then several years later I sat in on one of Bill's "Managing Management Time" seminars. Participants burst into laughter as they recognized the problems Bill discussed. Since crying in public is not an accepted practice, the only thing left for us to do was laugh. And laugh we did. Why? Because Bill Oncken, time after time, hit both the absurdities and realities of organizational life in America with such accuracy that it hurt.

Bill Oncken, more than anyone else, has taught me that if I really want to help others, I need to teach them how to fish rather than give them a fish. Taking the initiative away from people and caring for and feeding their monkeys is nothing more than rescuing them, that is, doing things for them they can do for themselves.

So when Hal Burrows, a longtime associate and principal of the William Oncken Company and one of the outstanding presenters of the "Managing Management Time" seminar, approached me about co-authoring this book, I was thrilled. In fact, I am honored to have this book as part of THE ONE MINUTE MANAGER LIBRARY.

Hal and I wrote several drafts of this book with Bill over about a three-year period. Then Bill suffered a serious illness and died as we were completing the final working draft of this book. So he never saw the finished publication. As I write these words my heart aches because of the loss of Bill. I am especially sad for those people who never knew Bill Oncken, for they suffer the greatest loss. My hope is that reading this book can soften that loss because it reads as accurately and humorously as Bill and colleagues like Hal Burrows have told thousands of managers about monkey management over the years. This is vintage Bill Oncken with the bite and insight left in.

What follows is a story about a harried manager who worked long, hard hours, yet never quite seemed to get caught up with all the work he had to do. He learned about monkey management and how not to take initiative away from his people so they can care for and feed their own "monkeys." In the process, he learned to be more effective in dealing with his own manager and the demands of his organization. The performance of his department drastically improved as did the prospects for his career.

*Bill Oncken's seminar and book, "Managing Management Time," include many wonderful insights about how organizations really function and present strategies for gaining the support of your boss, staff, and internal and external peers.* The One Minute Manager Meets the Monkey is *adapted from the "staff" strategy.*

My hope is that you will use what you learn in this book to make a difference in your life and the lives of the people you interact with at work and at home.

—Kenneth Blanchard, Ph.D
Co-author
*The One Minute Manager*

# This book is dedicated to the memory of William Oncken, Jr.

Bill Oncken, like Amadeus Mozart, was that exceedingly rare combination of masterful composer and virtuoso performer, the difference being that Bill used words instead of musical notes to fashion his works. His masterwork, *Managing Management Time*, is a timeless, enduring composition that captures the very essence of management, an art as old as organizations themselves. And anyone who ever saw him perform his work will never forget the experience!
—Hal Burrows

 *Contents*

IF you are someone who feels overwhelmed with problems created by other people, what you are about to read can change your life. It's the story of a manager, but it applies as well to other roles in life, especially parents and teachers.

This is the account of how my career went from imminent failure to considerable success after some wise counsel from two able people. My purpose in telling it here is to pass along their wisdom to you in the hope that it will help you as it has helped me.

The story begins some two years ago after a luncheon meeting with my friend, the One Minute Manager. I returned to my office, sat down at my desk, shook my head in amazement, and thought about what had just happened.

During lunch I had poured out my frustrations about my work. My friend listened and then told me the cause of my problems. I was astonished that the solution was so obvious.

What surprised me most was that the problem was self-inflicted. I guess that's why I couldn't see it without some help. But when my eyes were opened I realized that I was not alone; I knew other managers with the same problem.

As I sat there alone in my office I laughed aloud. "Monkeys!" I said to no one in particular. "I never would have suspected my problem is monkeys."

For the first time in a long time I remember smiling as I glanced at the picture on my desk of my wife and children. I began to look forward to enjoying more time with them.

About a year before the "monkey revelation" I had been appointed to my first management position. Things had started off well. I was initially very enthusiastic about my new work, and my attitude seemed to rub off on the people who reported to me. Productivity and morale gradually increased; both had been reported to be low before I took over as head of the department.

After the initial surge, however, the output of the department began to decline, slowly at first, then rapidly. The drop in performance was followed by a similar slide in morale. Despite long hours and hard work, I was unable to arrest the decline in my department. I was puzzled and very frustrated; it seemed that the harder I worked, the further behind I got and the worse the performance of my department became.

I was working extra hours every workday as well as Saturdays and some Sundays. I just never got caught up. There was pressure every minute, and it was extremely frustrating. I feared I was developing an ulcer and a nervous twitch!

I realized that all this was starting to wear a little thin with my family, too. I was so seldom home that my wife, Sarah, had to manage most of the family problems alone. And when I was home, I was usually tired and preoccupied with work, sometimes even in the middle of the night. Our two kids were also disappointed because I never seemed to have any time to play with them. But I didn't see any alternatives. After all, I had to get the work done.

My boss, Alice Kelley, had not been initially critical of me, but I began to notice a change in her behavior. She started asking for more reports on the performance of my department. She was obviously starting to watch things more closely.

ALICE seemed to appreciate the fact that I wasn't knocking on her door all the time asking for help. But at the same time she was more than a little concerned about the performance of my department. I knew I could not let things go on like that much longer. Consequently, I made an appointment to see her.

I told her I knew things had not been going well lately but I hadn't yet figured out how to improve the situation. I remember telling her my workload made me feel as if I were doing the work of two people. I'll never forget her reply: "Tell me who they are and I'll see that one of them is fired because I can't afford the overhead."

Then she asked me if perhaps I shouldn't be turning over more to my staff. My answer was that my staff was not ready to take on the additional responsibility. Again she responded in a way I'll never forget: "Then it's your job to get them ready! This situation is making me very nervous, and as Benjamin Franklin's grandfather once said:"

*

*It's Tough
To Work For
A Nervous Boss,
Especially
If You Are The One
Who's Making Your Boss
Nervous!*

*

AFTER my meeting with Alice, I thought a lot about what she had said. Those words "nervous boss" kept coming back to me. I began to realize that Alice was expecting me to handle this situation on my own, probably because she was extremely busy herself on a critical project. That's why I had called the One Minute Manager for help. He was a senior manager in another company and a longtime family friend. Everyone called him the "One Minute Manager" because he got such great results from his people with seemingly little time and effort on his part.

When we met at lunch, my problems must have shown on my face because the first thing he said was "So, being a manager is not as easy as you thought, eh?"

"That's an understatement," I answered. I lamented that back in the good old days before I became a manager things were a lot easier because my performance depended strictly on my own efforts. In those days, the longer and harder I worked the more I got done. "That formula seems to be working in reverse now," I told him.

As I went on to describe my problem in greater detail, the One Minute Manager just listened, only breaking his silence with an occasional question. His questions got more and more specific as the conversation continued. He asked me which aspect of my work was taking the biggest portion of my time.

I told him about an avalanche of paperwork in my office. "It's horrendous and getting worse." Sometimes it seemed that all I did was shuffle papers without ever making any progress on the real work that needed to be done; I labeled it *the triumph of technique over purpose*. It was a paradox— I was doing more but accomplishing less.

It seemed that everyone in the company needed something from me yesterday, things that might have been important to them but had little to do with getting my job done. And when I tried to focus on one matter, I would inevitably be interrupted to attend to another. I was spending more time in meetings and on the telephone. By the time I took care of all the paperwork, meetings, and interruptions, there was just no time left to implement some of the ideas I had for improving our own operation.

I told him I had even taken a seminar on time management. Frankly, I think the course made things worse. In the first place, attending it got me two days farther behind in my work. Moreover, even though it helped me become a bit more efficient, I think my increased efficiency merely made room for more work because no matter how much I did there was always more to do.

Then there was my staff. Wherever I saw them—in hallways, elevators, parking lots, cafeteria lines—there was always something they needed from me before they could proceed with their work; I guess that's why I had to work overtime and they didn't. If I left my office door open they were constantly streaming in, so I usually kept it closed. I regretted doing that because I was holding up their work and I suspected that was a big part of their morale problem.

The One Minute Manager listened carefully to my tale of woe. When I finally finished, he suggested that I seemed to be the victim of a fundamental management dilemma:

*

***Why Is It
That Some Managers
Are Typically
Running Out Of Time
While Their Staffs
Are Typically
Running Out Of Work?***

*

I thought that was an excellent question, particularly when I added up all the people in addition to my staff who were vying for my time. "But," I remarked, "perhaps I shouldn't complain about people needing me all the time. The way things have been going lately, being indispensable might be my only job security!"

The One Minute Manager disagreed sharply. He explained that indispensable managers can be harmful, not valuable, especially when they impede the work of others. Individuals who think they are irreplaceable because they are indispensable tend to get replaced because of the harm they cause. Moreover, higher management cannot risk promoting people who are indispensable in their current jobs because they have not trained a successor.

His explanation sent my thoughts back to my last conversation with my boss, who certainly didn't act as though I was indispensable. In fact, the more I thought about it, the more I realized that if I didn't soon resolve my problems our next conversation could be about career planning . . . for me! And why not? If I could not manage even my current small department, perhaps I shouldn't even be a manager.

IT was at that point during lunch that the One Minute Manager bowled me over with his astonishing (to me!) diagnosis of my problem. First he suggested that my attempts to solve the problem—working overtime, attending seminars— addressed merely the symptoms of the problem, not the cause itself. He said it was like taking an aspirin to reduce the fever but ignoring the illness that caused the fever. As a result, the problem had gotten progressively worse.

I remember thinking, "This is not what I want to hear, that all the work I've been doing has made the problem worse. After all, if I hadn't done the work I would be even farther behind."

I objected to my friend's diagnosis, but my argument soon fell by the wayside when his probing turned up the fact that the mission and staff of my department had not changed since my arrival—the only change *was* my arrival! An unsettling reality suddenly pried its way into my mind. To paraphrase Pogo, "I have seen the enemy, and he is I!"

Remembering that moment I often think about the story of a group of workers having lunch. They all had lunch boxes. One, when he opened his box and saw the contents, shouted, "Bologna sandwiches again! This is the fourth straight day I've had bologna sandwiches. And I don't like bologna!"

One of his co-workers said, "Relax! Relax! Why don't you ask your wife to pack some other kind of sandwich?"

"My wife, heck!" the worker said. "I made the sandwiches myself."

Since there seemed to be nowhere else to look for the source of the problem, I asked my friend to tell me more. He looked me straight in the eye and said, "Your problem is . . . MONKEYS!"

"Monkeys!" I laughed. "That sounds about right. My office usually seems like a zoo. What do you mean?" Then he gave me this definition of a monkey:

*

# A Monkey
# Is The Next Move

*

HE explained the definition with an example so vivid and true to life that I can quote it to you almost word for word to this day.

Let's say I am walking down the hall when I encounter one of my people, who says, "Good morning, boss. Can I see you for a minute? We have a problem." I need to be aware of my people's problems so I stand there in the hallway listening while he explains the problem in some detail. I get sucked into the middle of it, and, because problem-solving is my cup of tea, time flies. When I finally glance at my watch, what seemed like five minutes has actually been thirty.

The discussion has made me late for where I was headed. I know just enough about the problem to know I will have to be involved, but not yet enough to make a decision. So I say, "This is a very important problem, but I don't have any more time to discuss it right now. Let me think about it and I'll get back to you." And with that, the two of us part company.

"As a detached, perceptive observer," he continued, "it was probably easy for you to see what happened in that scenario. I assure you it is much harder to see the picture when you are in the middle of it. Before the two of us met in the hall the monkey was on my staff member's back. While we were talking, the matter was under joint consideration, so the monkey had one leg on each of our backs. But when I said, 'Let me think it over and get back to you,' the monkey moved its leg from my subordinate's back onto my back and my subordinate walked away thirty pounds lighter. Why? Because the monkey then had both legs on my back.

"Now, let us assume for the moment that the matter under consideration was part of my staff member's job. And let us further assume that he was perfectly capable of bringing along some proposed solutions to accompany the problem he raised. That being the case, when I allowed that monkey to leap onto my back I volunteered to do two things a person working for me is generally expected to do: (1) I accepted the responsibility for the problem from the person, and (2) I promised the person a progress report. Let me explain:

*

*For
Every Monkey
There Are Two
Parties Involved:
One To Work It
And One To Supervise It*

*

"In the instance just described, you can see that I acquired the worker role and my subordinate assumed the supervisory role. And just to make sure I know who's the new boss, the next day he will stop by my office several times to say, 'Hi, boss. How's it coming?' And if I have not resolved the matter to his satisfaction, he will suddenly be pressuring me to do what is actually his job."

I was dumbfounded. The One Minute Manager's vivid description of role reversal instantly triggered pictures in my mind of dozens of monkeys currently residing in my own office.

The most recent was a memo from Ben, a member of my staff, that said, in effect, "Boss, we're not getting the support we need from Purchasing on the Beta Project. Could you speak to their manager about it?" And, of course, I agreed. Since that time Ben had twice followed up on the matter with "How's it coming on the Beta Project? Have you spoken with Purchasing yet?" Both times I guiltily replied, "Not yet, but don't worry, I will."

Another was from Maria, who was requesting my help because I possessed (as she so astutely observed) "greater knowledge of the organization and of the technical peculiarities of certain problems" than she did.

Yet another monkey I had promised to handle was to write a job description for Erik, who had been transferred from another department to fill a newly created position in my department. I had not had time to specify exactly the duties of this new job, so when he asked me what was expected of him, I promised to write a job description to clarify his responsibilities.

My mind raced with a blur of monkeys and how I had acquired them. Two recent monkeys were in the form of incomplete staff work from Leesa and Gordon. I was planning to analyze the one from Leesa, note the areas that needed more work, and return it to her with suggested changes. The other, from Gordon, was back in my office for the fourth time; I was thinking of completing it myself rather than having to deal with him again.

Monkeys, monkeys, monkeys! I even had some *ricochet monkeys!* These monkeys were created by Maria, whose work and personal style sometimes caused problems for people in other parts of the organization. The other people then brought the problems to me for my invariable reply: "I'll look into it and get back to you."

As I thought about it, I realized that some of the monkeys were opportunities rather than problems. For example, Ben is a very creative person who is great at conceiving new ideas. But, to put it mildly, developing his ideas into finished products is not one of his strengths. So he sent me a series of suggestions which, though underdeveloped, had so much potential that I penned myself notes of things to do in order to capitalize on each of them.

As monkey after monkey scampered through my mind, I clearly saw that most of them should have been handled by my staff. But some of the monkeys belonged to me alone; that is, they were part of *my* job description. For example, when one of my people is sick or untrained or otherwise incapable of doing a task, I sometimes have to help out. And when emergencies arise, I sometimes handle monkeys my staff should handle if there were no emergency. Another example of monkeys that legitimately belong to me is the case where a member of my staff formulates a recommendation for handling a particular situation. Once that person gives the recommendation to me, then one or more of several "next moves" legitimately belong to me. I need to read the recommendation or listen to it being explained, question it, think about it, make a decision, react to it, and so on.

THE One Minute Manager confirmed my observation that some monkeys belong to me, but we both agreed, however, that by far the greatest proportion of the monkeys in my office at that time were those I should never have picked up.

You can easily imagine how this becomes a vicious cycle. When I picked up monkeys my people could have handled, they got the message that I *wanted* the monkeys. So naturally the more I picked up, the more they gave me. Soon I had as many as I could handle in a normal workday (given all the other requirements of my job from my boss and others), but the monkeys kept coming.

So I began "borrowing" time from my personal life: exercise, hobbies, civic activities, church, and eventually from my family. (I rationalized, "It's the quality, not the quantity, of the time with them that counts.")

I eventually reached the point where there was no more time available. But the monkeys still kept coming. That's when I started procrastinating. I was procrastinating and my staff was waiting. We were both doing nothing on the monkeys, a costly duplication of effort!

My procrastination made me a bottleneck to my staff; immobilized by me, they became bottlenecks to people in other departments. When those people complained to me, I would promise to look into the matters and get back to them. Time spent on these "sideward-leaping monkeys" further reduced the amount of time available for my staff's monkeys even more. Then my boss got wind that there might be problems in my department and started demanding more reports from me. These "downward-leaping monkeys" took precedence over all others, and time spent on them left even less time for the others. Looking back on that mess, I realize I was the cause of organizational gridlock; it is incredible how much trouble I caused.

Of course, the greater problem was that of "opportunity cost"; spending *all* my time working on other people's monkeys meant I had no opportunity to work on my own. I was not manag*ing*, I was being manag*ed*. I was not *pro*active, I was strictly *re*active. I was merely coping.

As we continued our lunch, the One Minute Manager and I talked mostly about the problems monkeys create in organizations. We were almost finished before it dawned on me that I was not at all sure what to do about this monkey business, so I confessed, "I admit it. I do have a huge menagerie of my staff's monkeys. But what can I do about it? And what can I do about the problems with my boss, and about the time-consuming demands of all the other people in the organization?"

He replied, "Many of those downward-leaping monkeys from your boss and those sideward-leaping monkeys from your peers are offspring of the upward-leaping monkeys from your staff. Once you correct this situation with your staff you'll have time to deal with those other two sets of monkeys. But this is not the time or place to discuss that process. The best way to learn about that is by attending a seminar called "Managing Management Time."

I reminded him that I had already taken a time-management course and the course only made things worse.

"Ah," he said, "but this seminar is different. The course you took focused on doing things right, which is okay, but it neglected to teach you the right things to do. You became more efficient, but you were doing the wrong things. You were like a pilot making great landings at the wrong airport. The seminar I'm recommending will help you learn:"

\*

# *Things Not Worth Doing Are Not Worth Doing Well*

\*

As we were leaving the restaurant I thanked the One Minute Manager for his help and promised I would make every effort to attend the seminar (secretly wondering how I could possibly take two days off from work!). Then I got the shock of my life when I asked him how he happened to know so much about this monkey management.

Grinning, the One Minute Manager answered, "Because I once had the same problem you do, only much, much worse. Like you, my career was in trouble and I was desperate. One day a brochure announcing a time-management seminar came across my desk. Like a drowning man grasping for a straw I decided to attend. It was lucky I did because that's where I learned all about monkey management!"

It was hard for me to believe that such a professional manager could ever have suffered from this problem. I asked him to tell me more, and the One Minute Manager did, with gusto.

"The course was taught by its creator, Bill Oncken. I'll never forget the spellbinding story he told that opened my eyes to the problem. It was a parable that paralleled my situation so closely it was eerie.

"Oncken told us how, like you and me, he'd been working long hours but still couldn't keep up. And how, as usual, he left home early one Saturday morning to go to work to get caught up, explaining to his disappointed wife and kids that his sacrifice was all for them. I almost cried when I heard him say that because I had uttered those very words the previous weekend.

"Oncken told us how he looked out his office window that Saturday morning to the golf course across the street and saw his staff there, getting ready to tee off. 'They were teeing up,' he said, 'and I was teed off! I became convinced that if, by magic, I could be transformed into a fly and buzz about their heads, I would overhear one of them remark to another: "Things are looking up, did you see whose car just pulled into the company parking lot? Looks like the boss has finally decided to earn his money!"'"

The One Minute Manager continued, "Then Oncken told us he looked down at that pile of papers on his desk and suddenly realized this was *their* work he was about to do. He was behind in their work, not his. He had never been behind in his work because he never had gotten it started! Then it hit him like a thunderbolt—'They're not working for me; I'm working for them! And with four of them generating work and only one of me working it off, I'll never get caught up by working harder because the more I do, the more they will give me!'

"Then," continued the One Minute Manager, obviously enjoying telling the story, "Oncken said, 'It suddenly hit me that I was way behind in some other things as well. So I ran out of my office and down the hall as fast as my legs would carry me. The weekend janitor, seeing me go by like a streak of lightning, asked where I was going in such a hurry. I yelled back that my speed was explained by where I was leaving from, not where I was going to.'

"Mr. Oncken related how he went down the stairs hitting every sixth step, jumped in his car and sped home. In the space of half an hour he had gone from the agony of facing two days of work to the thrill of spending two days with his family. He had a great weekend with his family and Saturday night he slept so soundly that twice during the night his wife thought he was dead.

"Yes," said the One Minute Manager, "Bill Oncken painted a perfect picture of me, a compulsive monkey-picker-upper. But thank goodness he showed us what to do about it, and my life has never been the same since. Nor will yours."

"I'll bet I know the title of the seminar you attended," I said. My friend smiled and nodded his agreement.

AFTER we parted, amazed at all I had heard, I returned to my office. When I walked in I saw monkeys everywhere. Where I had once seen backs of envelopes with notes written to myself, I now saw monkeys. (I have since given some thought to going into business selling pads of "backs of envelopes" to people like me.) Telephone messages were monkeys. (I pictured a monkey going through a telephone line like a pig passing through a python.) My briefcase appeared as a monkey cage. The note pad on my desk was a grappling hook, which I had so often used to pull monkeys off other people's backs.

As I looked around my office that day, my gaze settled on the picture of my wife and children and for the first time ever I realized *I have never been in the picture!* I resolved to correct that.

The family picture also reminded me that my wife and I pick up our kids' monkeys. Just recently my son came home and said to us, "Mom! Dad! I made the junior tennis team!"

We said, "Great! Isn't that wonderful. We're proud of you." Then he said, "There's only one problem: I need a ride to practice after school every Monday, Wednesday, and Friday, and then someone needs to pick me up when we're done." And who do you think got that monkey? My wife and I. What started as a celebration became a monkey.

What's worse is that the monkey quickly multiplied! My wife said to my son, "I could take you on Monday and some Fridays, but Wednesdays are a real problem for me. Who else is on your team so maybe I can set up a car pool?"

After my son told her who was on the team, she said, "I'll get on this right away, honey, and let you know who will be driving you." Without a care in the world, my son ran off to watch TV with a cheery, "Thanks, Mom."

OF course my son couldn't drive a car, but he certainly could have made an effort to arrange transportation alternatives and in the process learned to take some responsibility. Reliving that situation made me realize how easily we needlessly pick up other people's monkeys in all arenas of life. In the process, we neglect our own monkeys and make other people dependent upon us and deprive them of opportunities to learn to solve their own problems.

In retrospect, I can better understand the statements of General George C. Marshall, who said, "If you want someone to be for you, never let him feel he is dependent on you. Make him feel that you are in some way dependent on him," and Benjamin Franklin, who said, "The best way to convert a friend into an enemy is to get him indebted to you."

As I reviewed my luncheon discussion with the One Minute Manager, I realized he was concerned that I had become a "rescuer"—someone who was doing for others what they could do for themselves and in the process giving them the message they were "not okay." He told me that every time one of my people came to me and shared a problem and I took the monkey away from that person, what I was saying, in essence, was "You're not capable of handling this problem so I had better take care of it myself."

The One Minute Manager said that I was by no means alone in what I was doing. In fact, he implied it was almost becoming a disease in our country. He even had contemplated starting an organization called "Rescuers Anonymous" for people who were compulsive monkey-picker-uppers. It would be a gathering of "do-gooders"— very loving people who were running around trying to help others but who were crippling those they were trying to help by making them dependent. He said we have almost institutionalized rescuing in our government and throughout our society.

Then the One Minute Manager illustrated the depths of the rescuing mentality in this country by telling me his example of Little League. I can almost hear him now:

"When I was young, if we wanted to play baseball we had three problems. First of all, we needed equipment. In those days the one thing that guaranteed you would play was having a bat. There just weren't that many bats available then and if your bat broke, you'd never even think about running home and asking your parents to buy you a new one. Instead, you'd pound a few nails in it and wrap it with tape. I'll never forget running down to first base with my hands vibrating from one of those 'broken bats.'

"I also didn't know a baseball was white until I was nine—that's when we got our first TV. All the balls we used were covered with black tape. In fact, sometimes with a large ball you didn't know whether it was a softball or really a hardball that just had so much tape around it that it was the size of a softball. I just knew that some of the balls were so heavy that if you could hit a fly ball to the shortstop that was considered a 'long hit.'

"And gloves?" The One Minute Manager continued, "We didn't have that many then and I wasn't from a poor neighborhood. I can never remember running in from the field to bat when I didn't throw my glove to someone coming out to field. Today I know kids who have two or three different gloves.

"Once we got our equipment, the second problem was finding a place to play. If you lived in the city, you'd find a city block that didn't get much traffic and where residents could park their cars elsewhere. Then you would use the sewers, hydrants and the like for bases. If you lived in the country, as I did, you found a vacant lot or a farmer's field where you could clear off all the rocks except the four you were going to use for bases.

"The third and last problem, once we had equipment and a field," said the One Minute Manager, "was to find kids to play. Since we rarely had an abundance of kids, we had to choose from what was available. As a result, a team would range in age all the way from seven or eight to eighteen. I had real heroes when I was a kid. I remember that if Harry Haig even said 'hello' to me when I was a kid, I was thrilled. If he asked me to go to right field on defense, I never complained. Not even when a left-handed batter came up and he shouted for me to get in left field! I never ran home and told my parents I wasn't playing enough. I just knew if I was patient, when I got older I would get to pitch, catch, or play third base.

"After we had equipment, a field, and kids, we started hitting the ball around and playing choose-up games. Pretty soon we started thinking we were real good. Then someone would say, 'I understand Keith Dollar has a group that plays ball in his neighborhood.' So someone would see Dollar in school and challenge his team to a game. We'd play and beat them and then someone else would say, 'I understand Bill Bush has a group.' So we'd challenge them and beat 'em.

"We ended up having a six-team league when I was a kid: the Berrian Bombers, the Seacord Sissies, the Abafoil Asses and others like them. But who did all the planning? We did! Who did all the organizing? We did! And the motivating and controlling? We did!" exclaimed the One Minute Manager.

"And who does it today? The parents! All the kids have to do is get dressed. And do they get dressed! They all look like Joe DiMaggio or Willie Mays. And it's not just baseball—it's all youth sports. I remember working with a top manager in a Canadian company last year. In the middle of the afternoon he asked if I minded taking a drive with him to pick up his son so he could take him to youth hockey. We drove to his home and tooted the horn. The door opened and a kid came staggering out just loaded down with equipment. He was obviously a goalie. I asked, 'How old is he?,' since I couldn't tell.

"'Seven' was the answer. Halfway down the sidewalk the kid tripped and fell. If we hadn't gotten out of the car and helped him up he would have died there. With all that equipment on, there was no way he could have gotten up himself.

"I remember playing hockey as a kid on the lake in front of the high school," said the One Minute Manager. "We would spend all afternoon clearing the snow off the lake. Then, just about the time we finished and we were ready to play, our moms would come by and tell us to come home for dinner. That night it would snow again and we'd have to start clearing again the next day. When we finally got the ice cleared, we'd put two rocks at either end of our 'rink' to mark the goals. And if you played goalie then, and even hinted that you were wearing a 'jock,' they would call you a 'sissy.'

"After the kids get dressed today they get driven to the games. No one would want them to get any exercise. Once they get to the game, there are incredible fields with a refreshment stand where mothers and fathers are sweating, preparing hot dogs and hamburgers and all kinds of goodies. We certainly wouldn't want the kids to be hungry!

"Then there are parents sitting in the stands with major-league scorebooks scoring the game. When a kid hits one to third and the fielder throws him out, the poor parent has to figure what to write down as if this was the World Series.

"In the outfield there is a kid, sweating like mad, changing the scoreboard. When we were kids we kept score on the ground with a stick. One of the opponents would come over and say, 'You didn't get that run,' and would rub it out with his foot. Then you'd have to push him aside and scratch it in again.

"And the final straw," said the One Minute Manager, "when the game is over today and you lose, you can't even hassle the opponent! You have to go to Baskin-Robbins or Häagen-Dazs for ice cream. Have you ever tried to get ice cream on a Saturday afternoon? Every kid in town is in there, legions of little future major leaguers, yelling for some ice cream.

"As parents we have taken all the 'next moves' away from our kids. As a result, all the monkeys are on our backs, and the kids don't learn responsibility. In our well-intentioned desire to give them the good things we didn't have, we sometimes neglect to give them the good things we did have. Often kids today don't know what to do if nothing is planned," emphasized the One Minute Manager. "When I was a kid, if I told my mother I was bored, she would either give me a good swift kick in the pants and say, 'How's that for a little excitement?,' or say, 'That's great! Go clean out the garage.' We'd sure get over our boredom quickly."

WHAT I began to learn from the One Minute Manager, and continued to learn from the seminar he recommended was that the more I take care of everything for other people, the more dependent they become. In the process, their self-esteem and confidence are eroded and I am prevented from dealing effectively with my own monkeys.

Many of the monkeys in my office (mine and my staff's) were pitifully emaciated for lack of attention. I figuratively patted one of my staff's monkeys on the head and said, "Don't worry, little fellow, you'll be going home soon." Then with a glance at my own monkeys I said, "And I will finally have some time for you!"

A feeling of optimism came over me as I glanced up to my office wall at the poster my wife had given me some years ago. It showed a picture of Sir Isaac Newton sitting under a tree, having just been bopped on the head by a falling apple. The caption read:

*

*Experience
Is Not
What Happens
To You;
It's What
You Do
With
What Happens
To You*

*

AS I sat there in my office that Friday after lunch, I knew my life had just taken a sharp turn for the better. At the same time I had a sneaking suspicion that there was a lot more to learn. Nevertheless, I left my office early that day to enjoy a rare delightful weekend with my family. In fact, my minister expressed surprise at seeing me in church on an "off Sunday," which he explained was all except Easter. In the past he would always say on Easter Sunday, "Let me be the first to wish you a Merry Christmas!"

At this point I suppose you are wondering what happened to all those monkeys when I returned to my office on Monday morning after the weekend with my family. Very little, as it turned out, because, first, I didn't know what to do about them, and second, I spent the first three days of the week scrambling to get things arranged so I could attend the seminar the One Minute Manager recommended.

And attend I did! The "Managing Management Time" seminar was just as eye-opening an experience as the One Minute Manager said it would be. What I liked about it most was you could put what you learned into practice right away. I couldn't wait until the Monday after the seminar. That's when all the monkeys got what they deserved. I can assure you it was a day my staff and I will not soon forget.

As I drove to work that day, my mind was filled with delicious anticipation as I thought over the strategies and techniques I was about to apply with my staff. I could hardly wait to return my people's monkeys to their proper owners.

Heavy traffic that morning caused me to arrive about ten minutes late at my office, which was just enough time for my staff to assemble outside where they often performed their supervisory duties of checking on their monkeys.

As I walked past them into my office, both they and I sensed a profound change in the air. I, because I knew what was about to happen, and they because the smile on my face told them they didn't. They had never seen me smile like that on Monday morning. That sudden change in my behavior made them burp in chorus. (Sudden, drastic changes can make people nervous!)

I was smiling because I saw them in an entirely new light! I had long viewed them as a major *source* of my problems; suddenly that morning, I saw them as the major *solution* to my problem. I saw each of their backs as a repository for several monkeys.

As I walked into my office, Valerie, my secretary, saw me forget to do something I had not forgotten to do in years. I forgot to shut my door. That made *her* burp! (Please note that without speaking a word I had upset my entire staff!) When I shouted out to ask Valerie who was first to see me, she couldn't believe her ears. "You mean you actually want to see somebody?" she asked. Replied I, "I never wanted to see somebody so badly in all my life. Who's first?"

At that point, following the sequence recommended by our seminar instructor, I took the first step toward my recovery—returning my people's monkeys to them. Over the course of the morning I met with each member of my staff and followed virtually the same procedure with each. First I apologized for having been a bottleneck to them, and I promised them that things would never again be the same.

THEN I firmly attached my people's monkeys to *their* backs and sat back and enjoyed an exhilarating sight as each subordinate departed my office . . . several monkeys screwed squarely between the shoulder blades of their departing owner! And later that day I made it a point to ask each of my people the same question all of them had been asking me for so long: "How's it coming?" (This is "job enrichment" for managers!)

When the last of them left my office that morning I sat there, alone, reflecting on the things that had just come to pass. The most obvious was that my door was open for a change; even so, there were no people or monkeys in there with me. I had achieved privacy and accessibility at the same time! For the first time in a long time I had time for my people but they didn't have time for me. What an important learning:

\*

*The More You
Get Rid Of
Your People's
Monkeys,
The More Time
You Have For
Your People*

\*

That point was driven home by an incident that occurred a couple of days after the Monday when my people got all their monkeys back. I was in my office, alone, with the door open and my feet on my desk, thinking. I was thinking about the things I could do to clear the way so my people could do their things. (In a very real sense, I was working for them, but I was not doing their work!) At the same time, my people were working on their monkeys and I hadn't seen them in a couple of days. Frankly, I was lonely! I didn't feel needed anymore.

As luck would have it, just then Erik came to see me about a problem. As he approached my office he noticed that my door was open. But from where he was standing he couldn't see me in there. Never had he seen my door open when I was in my office, so he must have assumed I was away on a trip. When he asked Valerie where I was, she said, "He's right in there." Erik was so shocked he stammered, "Well, uh, when could I see him?" Valerie replied, "Just go right on in. He's just sitting there. He isn't doing anything!"

When he came in I realized how lonely I had been. I greeted him warmly: "Come on in. Have a seat. I'm so glad to see you. How about some coffee? Let's start at the beginning. How are your wife and kids these days?" Erik's reply told me that my greeting was perhaps a bit more effusive and time-consuming than he felt was called for under the circumstances. Shaking his head he said, "I don't have time for that kind of B.S.!" *For once I had more time for him than he had for me!*

My staff knew, as does anyone who's ever experienced it, how frustrating it is to work for a boss who has no time for them. So now I endeavor always to have more time for them than they have for me. That is accomplished by expanding the amount of time I have for them and contracting the amount of time they have for me. I keep tabs on how I'm doing in this regard by always noting who runs out of time first each time I meet with a member of my staff; if they are running out of time more often than I am, that's a good indicator of their increasing self-reliance.

Consequently, I have developed the reputation among my staff as the most accessible manager they have ever known. They can see me as often as they wish (which is not very often) and for as long as they wish (which is not very long). This is a vast change from the time before my "conversion."

Moreover, once my people regained control of their monkeys that Monday, they were empowered to act. Thus they were no longer frustrated waiting for *me* to act, nor was I guilty because I owed them responses that I didn't have time to make. I was no longer an impediment to them as when I had their monkeys stacked in my office. In the space of a few hours I had gone from being indispensable (that is, my people couldn't make a move until I did) to being dispensable. As I learned, indispensable bosses are dangerous to organizations; thus they tend to get replaced. But bosses who are not impediments to their people can die and not even be missed, and bosses who can die and not be missed are so rare they are virtually irreplaceable. Why?

As a manager, to the extent that you can get people to care for and feed their own monkeys, they are really managing the work themselves. That frees up your discretionary time to do planning, coordinating, innovating, staffing, and other key managerial tasks that will keep your unit functioning well into the future.

Now, having gotten this far on Monday, let's put matters into the proper perspective. What I have done so far is return my people's monkeys to them in accordance with Oncken's Rules of Monkey Management. Now let me tell you all about those rules!

## Oncken's Rules of Monkey Management

The dialogue between a boss and one of his or her people must not end until all monkeys have:

Rule 1. *Descriptions:*
The "next moves" are specified.

Rule 2. *Owners:*
The monkey is assigned to a person.

Rule 3. *Insurance Policies:*
The risk is covered.

Rule 4. *Monkey Feeding and Checkup Appointments:*
The time and place for follow-up is specified.

The purpose of the rules of monkey management is to help ensure that the *right things* get done the *right way* at the *right time* by the *right people*.

Monkey rules are crucial if you think back to some of the problem-solving meetings you've attended. Most of those meetings ended without everyone in the room agreeing *what* the "next moves" were to be, *when* they were to be made, and *who* was responsible for making them.

The problem with such meetings is that if no one knows what the "next move" is, it can't be made. Also, if no one has been assigned responsibility for it, then it becomes everybody's responsibility (or rather, nobody's responsibility), which raises the odds nothing will be done. And even if a "next move" is specified and assigned to someone, if there is no deadline attached, the odds of procrastination are increased because we are all too busy with urgent matters to spend time on matters that can be put off.

The rules of monkey management should be applied only to monkeys that deserve to live. Some do not. Some monkeys are in the same category as the British civil-service job that consisted of standing atop the white cliffs of Dover and ringing a bell if Napoleon's troops started across the English Channel—a job that was filled until 1948. So always ask yourself: "Why are we doing this?" If there is no viable answer, shoot the monkey so that you won't be doing more efficiently things that should not be done in the first place.

IN order to understand and apply the rules of monkey management, it will help to bear in mind the definition of a monkey. Remember, the monkey is not a project or a problem; *the monkey is whatever the "next move" is* on a project or problem.

Rule 1 means that *a boss and a staff member shall not part company until appropriate "next moves" have been described.* Some examples of monkey descriptions are: "Obtain final cost figures from accounting," "Prepare a sales proposal," "Give the matter further thought," "Formulate a recommendation," and "Get the contract signed."

There are three principal benefits of adhering to this rule. First of all, if my people know in advance that the dialogue between them and me will not end until appropriate "next moves" have been described, they will tend to do *more careful planning before our dialogue begins*. My boss, Alice, taught me this lesson long ago. One day I was bending her ear about all my problems, and I asked her what I should do. She said, "You mean you don't know what to do?" I told her I didn't, so she said, "Well, I don't know what you should do, either. That makes two of us who don't know what you should do, and the company can afford only one of us!"

That was her way of reminding me that for every problem or opportunity brought to her attention, I should also bring some thoughtful recommendations for the "next moves" to be made on the situation. That way we wouldn't have to stand there in the hallway and do the thinking that I should have done before we talked.

The second benefit of Rule 1 is that it *biases any situation toward action by your people*. Many situations are biased toward paralysis, and no progress can be made until someone makes a "next move." For instance, when a problem or opportunity first arises, often the best solution is not immediately apparent, and often the potential hazards of the situation are not obvious. In those cases (especially if there is a lot at stake) it's so tempting for a boss to protect himself or herself by grabbing the monkey. . . . "Let me think about it and I'll get back to you." That leaves the staff member and the entire project on hold until the boss takes action; the person's initiative has been taken away by the boss. On the other hand, if the "next moves" are clearly described during the dialogue, it often becomes apparent that the subordinate can safely handle many of them, for example, "Give the matter some thought and study" and/or "Formulate a recommendation based on what is known to date." That way the situation doesn't stay in limbo until the boss gets around to doing something about it.

The third and probably the greatest benefit of adhering to Rule 1 is that specifying "next moves" can provide a *quadruple boost in motivation* for the owner of the monkey. First, describing the monkey *clarifies* the "next move," and the more clearly one understands what must be done, the greater the energy and motivation that exist for doing it. (Think about how hesitant you feel about making a move on some vexing problem when you have only a hazy idea of what to do.) Second, specifying the "next move" increases motivation by helping one take the all-important *first step* on a project, which is often the most difficult one to make. After the first step things usually seem easier. Third, specifying "next moves" breaks the project into *bite-size* pieces, and it is much less daunting to think about making a single "next move" on a project—for example, making a phone call—than to worry about all the effort required to complete the entire project. Fourth, describing "next moves" increases motivation by allowing one to *switch his focus* back and forth from goals to "next moves." If the goal—completing the entire project—seems overwhelming, thinking about the "next move"—making a call—is less so; if thinking about all the "next moves" is discouraging, thinking about the satisfaction of achieving the final goal is less so.

Let me relate a couple of instances from my own experience to illustrate the value of the first rule of monkey management. For example, recall the definition of a monkey: *A monkey is the "next move."* This definition does not say anything about ownership. Therefore, it is possible that *one person can own the project and another person can make the "next move."* I often make use of this reality by asking various members of my staff what "next moves" I should make on certain projects of mine. That gives them the "next move" of formulating a recommendation to help me handle my project. This not only synergistically improves the quality of whatever "next move" I make (two heads are better than one even if they only add up to 1.3!), it also develops my people's abilities, and it gives them some insight into the challenges I face. And it helps train my successor (no small matter if I want a promotion).

Another example of using Rule 1 occurs when one of my people and I are discussing a situation and time runs out before we can even finish defining the problem, much less identifying and describing substantive "next moves." Running out of time means the "next move" is to babysit the monkey, i.e., to maintain responsibility for the matter at hand until the discussion is resumed. So I say to the person, "Why don't we talk about this again in a couple of days. In the meantime, you hold on to the problem in case you come up with an idea . . . and I hope you will!"

In the two ensuing days I probably would have done nothing about the monkey, and it is conceivable that my staff member might do *nothing*, too. But if nothing is going to be done, better it be done in her briefcase than mine. Why? Well, for one thing, it's dark inside a briefcase, so the monkey neither knows nor cares whose briefcase it's in. Also, if the monkey is in one of my people's briefcases it is at least conceivable that *something* might get done about it. And even if the *something* amounts to next-to-nothing, that's infinitely more than the nothing I would have done in the same amount of time! Furthermore, even if the *something* is wrong, that's of some value; there are only a finite number of ways to do a thing wrong and she just eliminated one of them!

Here's a final example describing the value of requiring "next moves." Let's say you and a staff member discuss an issue and the dialogue ends with your asking for a recommendation to resolve it. You smile as the two of you part company; *he* has the "next move," which is to formulate the recommendation.

But your pleasure ends with the arrival of his recommendation, a nine-pager, in your "In" basket. Now *you* have the "next moves": read it, think about it, decide what to do about it, do something about it, and so on. You have the worker role and he the supervisory role.

You can see from this scenario that in monkey business, as in chess and checkers, it pays to think ahead several moves. I have learned to avoid the monkeys just described by having my people *bring* me memos instead of sending them. Why? That way, when the person bearing the memo arrives in my office, I ask him or her to read the memo to me. (Several have indicated they could tell me about the memo in one-third the time it would take to read it, which makes me glad I didn't take the time to read the other two thirds!)

Whether they read it or tell me about it, I have time to think, to watch their facial expressions, and to ask questions. That helps me gain quicker and better understanding than if I had read it myself in isolation, because the memo, being composed of words, is subject to misinterpretation. Also, there is less information *in* the lines of the memo than *between* the lines, and the person who knows the most about what's between the lines is now sitting in front of me to answer any questions I might have.

THERE are countless way to apply Rule 1, but I'm sure you understand the approach by now. So let's move ahead to the next rule, which has to do with assigning ownership of monkeys.

Rule 2 of monkey management states that *the dialogue between boss and staff member must not end until ownership of each monkey is assigned to a person.* This rule is based on several thousand years of human experience that teach us that people take better care of things they own than things they don't. Also, if ownership of the monkey is not specified, nobody assumes personal responsibility for it and it follows that nobody can be held accountable for it.

Thus, the welfare of valuable organizational monkeys demands that they be owned by someone. Therefore, when I and one of my people are discussing a work-related issue, every monkey generated in that discussion must be assigned to one or the other of us before the dialogue ends.

But which monkeys go with whom? I have learned that:

\*

*All
Monkeys
Must Be Handled
At The Lowest
Organizational Level
Consistent With
Their Welfare!*

\*

Keeping the monkeys at the lowest possible level is not, as some view it, buck-passing or abdication of responsibility. On the contrary, there are powerful, legitimate reasons for doing so: (1) my staff has more collective time, energy, and, in many cases, more knowledge for handling monkeys than I do (managers who think they can outperform their entire staff are suffering *delusions of adequacy*), (2) my staff members are closer to their work than I am and are thus in a better position to handle their monkeys, and (3) keeping other people's monkeys out of my office is a key way to preserve some of my own discretionary time.

Consequently, since my "conversion" I have learned to retain *only* the monkeys that *only* I can handle—the rest of them go to my staff. I know there is a limit to how many monkeys my people can handle, so I work hard at making sure they feel free to tell me when they feel they are at their limits (as long as they bring along some recommendations for correcting their problems). But experience has also taught me that my people can often do more than I think they can, and they can sometimes do more than *they* think they can!

If you think as you read this that the practice of pushing monkeys down to the lowest prudent level is easier said than done, I agree. Being a reformed compulsive monkey-picker-upper myself, I am as aware as anyone that there are powerful forces pushing and pulling the monkeys upward.

Hindsight has revealed to me many of the reasons monkeys naturally leap upward. In my case, it was my internal personal needs that, like bananas in a tree, literally lured monkeys upward. The principal reason was that I enjoyed handling my staff's work far more than I enjoyed management. After all, I used to do that kind of work before I became a manager, and I was good at it. (That's why I got promoted!) So doing their work gave me a holiday from the challenges of management (this phenomenon is sometimes referred to as the "executive sandbox" syndrome), and at the same time doing their work provided my staff an opportunity to watch "genius at work"!

Even if I had been aware of all the real reasons I was picking up my staff's monkeys, I don't think I could have admitted them at the time. I now realize that I had concocted an elaborate collection of rationalizations (intellectually respectable, ego-serving reasons for doing things I had no business doing) for picking up monkeys. Have you ever heard any of the following? "If you want it done right you have to do it yourself." "You just can't get good help these days." "This one is just too hot for my staff to handle." "My boss expects me to do this one." "I just want to keep my hand in." "It's easier to do it than to delegate it." "I don't want to ask my people to do anything I'm not willing to do myself."

It is not only internal personal needs that send monkeys to the wrong owners; sometimes organizational policies do it. Some companies are finding, for example, that when the responsibility for product quality is taken away from those who produce the product and given to inspectors, that monkey is on the wrong back. The final product isn't nearly as defect-free. Given these personal and organizational forces, keeping monkeys with their proper owners requires a mixture of both skill and discipline, especially discipline, for without it skill is superfluous.

Great discipline is needed to overcome the following *apparent* paradox in management: Sometimes when you insist on the very best in your people's work, you may encounter resistance because doing their very best often requires hard work. On the other hand, if you permit your people to be less than their best, they sometimes don't actively resist. So it sometimes *seems* that they would rather do less than their best.

The dynamics of that apparent paradox work against the practice of keeping monkeys with their proper owners because it is sometimes easier to pick up the monkeys than to deal with the problems of keeping them on the backs of their rightful owners. But, beware . . . the paradox is only apparent, not real, as the great managers and leaders of history have taught us.

The leaders we remember most appreciatively are those who knew that in the long run other people, despite their apparent resistance, will respect you—even love you—if you help bring out the best in them.

To strengthen your resolve in this regard, think back to your school days. Which teachers do you remember most fondly? The ones I remember best were a few taskmasters who pushed me to the limit to do my best. And did I ever resist the pressure! At times I thought I hated them. (I think I sometimes prayed for their deaths!) But I did my best for them because deep down I knew they had my best interests at heart. Now I appreciate them above all the others, some of whom I don't even remember. In fact, I have found myself at times resenting those people who let me waste part of my life even though it was my own fault.

I demand excellence from myself and I expect no less from my staff. I still get some resistance when I challenge them to their limits. If they resist, I listen to them, but I keep in mind the example of my teachers and some of the other great managers I have known and heard about. When they resist, I recall the story of the farmer who, when asked by his neighbor why he was working his sons so hard just to grow corn, replied, "I'm not just growing corn. I'm growing sons!"

Remember:

*

*The Best Way
To Develop
Responsibility In People
Is To Give Them
Responsibility*

*

Now that you have some ideas about the *discipline* required to keep monkeys with their proper owners, I want to tell you about a few of my experiences that will help you improve your *skill* in applying the second rule of monkey management.

Before I learned these things, one of my people, Gordon, was a veritable monkey factory! Every time I saw him—in hallways, cafeteria lines, elevators, parking lots—his first words to me were "We've got a problem." Almost invariably I wound up with the monkey, and usually it was *his* monkey.

Since then, I have learned to avoid the care and feeding of Gordon's monkeys by using an *anti-straddle reflex* that is instantly provoked by the word "we." When I hear the phrase "We've got a problem" I visualize a straddling monkey with one leg on my back and the other on Gordon's back. Then I remember the dangers of this posture . . . the monkey might get a hernia, and I might get somebody else's monkey! That mental picture triggers an instantaneous and automatic response in my central nervous system.

I say to Gordon, "*We* do not have a problem, and *we* will never again have one. I'm sure there is a problem, but it is not ours, it is either yours or mine. The first item on the agenda is to neaten up the pronouns and find out whose problem this is. If it turns out to be my problem, I hope you will help me with it. If it turns out to be your problem, I will help you with it subject to the following condition: at no time while I'm helping you with your problem will your problem become my problem, because the minute your problem becomes my problem, you will no longer have a problem and I can't help a person who does not have a problem!"

By the time I finish my little speech the person wonders why he even brought it up. He figures he would be better off solving the problem himself than listening to me. But after the shock subsides we discuss the problem. Then we identify "next moves." I assign as many as possible to him and retain only those that are rightfully mine.

This process has taught Gordon, my "monkey factory," that the monkey can be owned by only one person, and that *he* owns it until the facts prove otherwise, and that the burden of proof is on him. For me to assume the burden of proof would be to pick up a monkey I should not have. That way the monkey never begins the straddle; it stays on Gordon's back until rightful ownership has been ascertained.

If Gordon convinces me it's my monkey, I calmly and deliberately reach over and take it; if it turns out to be his monkey, I don't have to delegate it because I don't have it—he still has it! Nowadays the phrase "We've got a problem" is seldom heard around my department.

In another instance, sheer paralysis on my part taught me a valuable lesson about keeping monkeys with their proper owners. It began when one of my people, Leesa, said to me, "Boss, *I've* got a problem." I replied, "A problem? Be positive. There's no such thing as problems. Just opportunities!" She replied, "In that case, I've got an insurmountable opportunity." After a good laugh, I asked her, "What's the problem?"

Leesa described her problem, but she offered no solutions. She stood there silently; I suppose she was waiting for me to tell her what to do. At that time I was so new at monkey management I didn't know what to say or do, so I stood there, stone silent, trying to figure out what to do next. The silence grew longer. I was uncomfortable. I don't know what Leesa was thinking, but finally she broke the silence by blurting out, "Why don't I think this thing over a little longer. I'm sure I can come up with something."

The discomfort of the silence caused Leesa to identify the monkey, assume and acknowledge ownership of it, and beat a hasty retreat! Although I learned that technique by accident, I have used it to good effect on other occasions. I have also learned other variations of it; in addition to silence, the discomfort that stimulates a person to snatch the monkey and run can be caused by a full bladder after several cups of coffee, or by a meeting that goes on past quitting time.

I am reminded of the story I once read about how a famous person handled the problem of upward-leaping monkeys in the form of incomplete work from one of his people. This staff member had not responded to any of the normal remedies, so the manager decided to try something drastic. The very next time he received an incomplete proposal from this person, he returned it with a note saying, "You're better than this!" The subordinate improved and resubmitted the proposal only to get it back the second time with another note: "Is this the very best you can do on this?" Again the person improved the proposal. This time he personally delivered it to his boss and said, "This is absolutely the best I can do on this matter," whereupon his boss replied, "Good. Now I'll read it."

W ELL, that's it for Rule 2, assigning ownership of monkeys. Now that they are on the proper backs, let's get the little buggers insured before we send them out to face the dangers of the organizational jungle.

Rule 3 of monkey management states that *the dialogue between boss and staff member shall not end until all monkeys have been insured*. This rule provides a systematic way to balance your staff's need for freedom in handling their monkeys with, simultaneously, your responsibility for the outcome.

Giving your people authority and freedom benefits both you and them. The benefit to you is discretionary time—the more freedom they have, the less of your time and energy is required to supervise them. At the same time, freedom allows your people to enjoy the many benefits of self-management (more satisfaction, more energy, higher morale, and the like).

But every benefit has its costs. The cost of giving your people more freedom is the increased risk that freedom entails. When people have freedom, they will make mistakes. Monkey insurance is designed to make sure they make *only affordable mistakes*! That is why all monkeys must be insured by one of the following policies:

# MONKEY INSURANCE POLICIES

### 1. RECOMMEND, THEN ACT
### 2. ACT, THEN ADVISE

Level 1, *Recommend, Then Act*, provides insurance in situations where I feel there is a reasonable risk that one of my people might make an *un*affordable mistake if left to his or her own devices. In such cases, where I think my staff's actions might "burn the building down," I want a chance to blow out the match beforehand, that is, I want a chance to veto their proposed actions. Such anxieties are usually connected with matters so important that if they were botched, I could not fire the botcher for incompetence because I myself would no longer have the authority. On these matters I require my people to formulate recommendations that I must approve *before* they can proceed any further. This provides protection, but at the cost of more of my time and some of my people's freedom.

Level 2 insurance, *Act, Then Advise*, is for monkeys I'm pretty sure my people can handle successfully on their own. They are free to resolve these matters and inform me afterward at whatever time they think is appropriate. This gives them a lot of operating room and saves me a lot of supervisory time. The risk is that if they take an action that is going to burn the building down I won't learn about it until afterward, when it is too late to do anything but hose down the ashes.

Who selects the insurance policy for a given situation? Although I, as manager, must ultimately *approve* all selections, either party might *make* the selection depending on the circumstances. Sometimes I make the selection, especially when I require the protection afforded by Level 1. My people sometimes complain a little when I choose Level 1 because it limits their freedom, but it would be abdicating my responsibility as a manager for me to allow them to operate on their own with Level 2 insurance when there is a significant risk of an unaffordable mistake.

Of course, it is neither possible nor desirable for me to tell my people in advance which policy to use on each and every thing they do. So, on most endeavors they assume the responsibility—and the risk!—of selecting the policy themselves (with the understanding that their selections must ultimately satisfy me). They elect to use Level 2 only when, in their judgment, they believe that it will be acceptable to me if they go ahead and handle the situation in their own manner and inform me later. Otherwise, they give me their recommendations in advance and then proceed with whatever actions we agree to in the dialogue (Level 1). If I am not satisfied with the policy they are using, I have the prerogative to change it. My aim is to:

*

*Practice
Hands-Off Management
As Much As
Possible
And
Hands-On Management
As Much As
Necessary*

*

I do this by *encouraging* my people to utilize Level 2 insurance as much as possible and *requiring* them to use Level 1 insurance as much as necessary.

Insuring monkeys is a dynamic process. A person will do some parts of his work with Level 1 authority and other parts with Level 2 authority. What is done with one level of insurance today might later require another level if circumstances change. In the following examples you will see the policies changing, sometimes on the discretion of my people and sometimes on my discretion.

The first example is the case of one of my former employees, Alex, who exercised more freedom than my anxieties would tolerate. He preferred to handle all his monkeys on a Level 2 basis and inform me only occasionally of what he was doing, seemingly immune to my requests to keep me better informed.

One day there was a huge problem with one of his projects. My boss found out about it before I did and expressed her displeasure to me in unmistakable terms. I went straight to Alex's office and did the same thing to him. I told him about how his not keeping me informed led to the unpleasant surprise I had just endured in my boss's office. I was furious. "All I'm asking is that you keep me informed, but you never do. But we'll fix that! From now on, don't do anything on this project until you check with me first."

Perhaps I overreacted, but nevertheless, Alex was the case of someone whose actions were such that my anxieties could not tolerate them at the time. In order to get my anxieties down to a level that allowed me to sleep at night, I had to move him back from Level 2 authority to Level 1. He complied, but, as you might suspect, he eased himself back into Level 2 after I calmed down and the project stabilized.

That was a case where someone exercised too much freedom; the next example has to do with an occasion where I *gave* one of my people too much freedom. Maria was somewhat anxious about a certain project and wouldn't make any substantial moves on it without checking with me first. She was using Level 1 insurance to get my fingerprints on everything she did. I was sure she could handle this project without checking with me so often, so I assured her of my confidence and asked her to resolve the matter on her own and let me know what she had done.

After Maria left my office I got a little concerned that if she was so anxious about the project, perhaps I should be, too. I began wondering if I had overlooked something important. I called her back and asked what was the worst thing that could go wrong with this project and what were the odds it would go wrong? Her answer almost gave me a heart attack! My knees turned to water. I was sweating. My hands were trembling.

I was petrified! Two years earlier, my fears would have caused me to yank that monkey off Maria's back, clutch it to my chest, and handle it myself. This time, however, I increased my protection by merely reinsuring it from Level 2 to Level 1. I told Maria, "On second thought, please let me know your plans before you take any further action on this matter." Then I slumped back into my chair, exhausted but relieved that I had caught the situation in time.

Later, as the project settled down and both Maria and I grew more comfortable with it and with each other, on her own discretion she moved to Level 2 authority on most aspects of it.

As it turned out, though, that project later became so important that my boss, Alice, began keeping closer tabs on it. One day she called to ask how it was going and I told her I was letting Maria handle most of it on her own (Level 2) because she had earned the right to do so and because I wanted to let her grow and shine. My boss told me that because of the customer involved, she wanted me to handle the matter personally. When I tried to dissuade her she told me something that really summed up the philosophy of balancing people's desire for freedom with the organization's need for protection: "I appreciate what you're doing," she said, "but this project is too risky for that. There will be other opportunities for developing your people." She told me to remember . . .

*

*Never
Let The Company
Go Down The Drain
Simply
For The Sake Of
Practicing
Good Management*

*

THE output of any organization is the sum of a myriad of "next moves," which means that the success of a company is a function of the health of its monkeys. Because monkey health is so vital, monkeys *must* have periodic checkups to maintain their well-being. That is the reason for Rule 4 of monkey management, which states that *the dialogue between boss and staff member shall not end until the monkey has a checkup appointment.*

Since monkeys sometimes develop unexpected problems, checkups are crucial. Wise people, even if they are healthy, schedule regular medical checkups in order to detect problems and correct them. Likewise with monkeys. If the checkup reveals problems, a treatment is devised. However, if the checkup shows the monkey to be in good health, good news is in order for its owner. So the purpose of monkey checkups is twofold: one, to catch people doing something right and praise them for it, and two, to spot problems and take corrective action before the problems become crises. The process of discovering and correcting problems tends to (1) lower the boss's anxieties, and (2) develop people's competence through coaching—which increases the boss's confidence in their competence and further decreases his or her anxieties, and (3) the coaching increases the odds that the boss will eventually be able to delegate to that person.

That is why no monkey leaves my office on the back of one of my people until the date for its checkup has been set. I prefer to minimize the number of *scheduled* checkups, so I like to schedule appointments as far in the future as would be advisable *if* the monkey were to receive no checkups in the interim. However, I have an understanding with my people that if anything arises in the meantime that makes either them or me nervous about the health of a monkey, either of us may take the initiative to move up the monkey's checkup appointment to an earlier time.

Here is an example of a monkey malady and of why rescheduled checkups are occasionally necessary. Sometimes when I am walking around keeping myself informed and letting my people know I am interested in them and what they are doing, I might notice a monkey that looks sick (it is suffering either malnutrition from lack of attention, or some illness from improper treatment). The monkey's problem is seldom the result of laziness, carelessness, malice, or anything like that; it is usually sick because my people, like all busy people, have to set priorities, and when they do, the monkeys at the bottom of the list sometimes suffer. And usually the reason they have not already told me about the monkey is because most of my people would rather solve their own problems than bring them to me . . . *which can be a problem in itself!*

For example, Erik, a member of my staff, is an extremely competent, diligent person who is so highly self-reliant that he will do his best to nurse an ailing monkey back to health before getting me involved. Such self-reliance is commendable unless taken to the extreme. Erik takes it to the extreme. He would not even inform me that the monkey had a tummy ache (much less ask for my help) until the poor creature was nearly beyond saving. Then my office would become an emergency room where I would have to drop everything else I was doing in order to deal with the crisis. In a sense, a routine appendectomy became a ruptured appendix with massive infection simply because I had not been informed a little earlier.

Before I learned better I would show my displeasure at such developments by giving Erik a lecture on the importance of monkey health, and ranting and raving because he had allowed the situation to degenerate. I have since learned two much more constructive ways to head off most crises and show my concern for monkeys.

One is developing an understanding between my people and me that they will treat their sick monkeys' maladies as best they can, but if the condition persists or worsens and does not respond to treatment, the monkey will be brought to my office for a checkup in time for me to get involved *before* its vital signs have disappeared.

In other words, if someone like Erik can't heal the monkey, and if there is a chance the little dear might not survive until the next scheduled checkup, it is Erik's responsibility to initiate an interim, precautionary checkup.

On the other hand, if I discover the malady, I deal with it by simply moving the next checkup appointment to a time warranted by the condition of the monkey. For example, if the sick monkey had been previously scheduled for a checkup in my office three weeks hence, I change that time to twenty-four hours hence. That sends a powerful message about my concern for the monkey.

An interesting example of this takes place when a monkey is in jeopardy due to inattention by its owner, that is, *something* should have been done about it but because *nothing* has been done, the project is in trouble. In that case, I move up the checkup appointment appropriately. Sometimes the person will request more time before the new checkup in order to get something done on the monkey. The reasoning, as some have explained, is that since nothing has been done, there is nothing to discuss during the checkup. But there is something very important to discuss—the fact that nothing has been done and the implications of that fact!

Moreover, if I give people more time because they have done nothing, I will reward their doing nothing, and what I reward I will get more of! In other words, if I allow the rendering of accountability to be delayed until whenever my people might happen to be ready, the monkey could starve or get sicker in the meantime.

So my response is that we will conduct the checkup anyway and discuss the "nothing" that has been done. This leaves the person facing two unpleasant courses of action: one, continue doing *nothing* and come into my office the next day and make a "lack of progress" report, or, two, do *something* and bring me a progress report. The result is predictable: my staff member digs in and progress on the monkey is miraculously made. A progress report made under conditions just described might be superficial the first time, but think about what the person learns with respect to handling future occasions. Anyway, *my* moving up a monkey's checkup appointment because *I* discovered it was starving to death is, in itself, a monkey I should never have in the first place.

The examples just described had to do with sick monkeys. An opposite problem occurs when the monkey is quite healthy and vigorous but is not the kind of monkey I envisioned when it was born. For example, not too long ago I was discussing a project with Ben, one of my people. We discussed the general aspects of the design, budget, and timing. I was sure we had achieved a good understanding about *what* was to be done so I largely left it up to him as to *how* to do it.

But the next time I checked on the matter, the design had gone off in a whole new direction and the potential cost of the project had gone through the roof, all of which was totally unacceptable to me. There can be many causes of such a problem: misunderstanding, conditions that change along the way, Ben's belief that his new design is better than what we agreed on, and so on. Periodic checkups tend to highlight the existence of such problems and limit their costs by allowing a manager to detect the problem and see to it that it is corrected.

Now a final note about checkup appointments. I used to be extremely reluctant to perform checkups on monkeys because I did not differentiate between checking up on monkeys and checking up on people. I thought checkups were the equivalent of snooping on people and assuming they would not do good work unless prodded by me. Since then, however, I have come to understand that checkups focus more on the monkeys' condition than on the people themselves, so checkups give me the opportunity to "catch people doing something right," detect and correct problems with monkeys, coach my people, reduce my anxiety level, and the like. After that, my people take care of their performance themselves (this is why managing monkeys properly means you don't have to manage people so much).

Because monkey checkups are so vital, they must be treated with great respect by both bosses and staff. And if the boss treats them as important, the staff will tend to do so as well. Therefore, I do anything I can to emphasize to my people the importance of checkup appointments. For example, when we schedule a checkup appointment, I make a point of writing it on my calender; *writing* the date gives the appointment more legitimacy and value than merely stating it. And if I am going to be late for an appointment, I make every effort to let my people know in advance. That not only illustrates the importance I attach to checkups, it also shows that I value punctuality as well.

Doing those things shows what I stand for and, by implication, *what I won't stand for*. People need to know both. So, for example, if one of my people is late or absent for an appointment and could have informed me in advance but didn't, I make things a little unpleasant. I deliver a little speech about how the next time he or she is unable to keep an appointment a call from the hospital will be cheerfully accepted. I rarely have to make this speech with any of my people anymore.

Now, having come this far, let's summarize the four rules of monkey management:

## A SUMMARY OF ONCKEN'S FOUR RULES OF MONKEY MANAGEMENT

Rule 1. *Describe the Monkey:* The dialogue must not end until appropriate "next moves" have been identified and specified.

Rule 2. *Assign the Monkey:* All monkeys shall be owned and handled at the lowest organizational level consistent with their welfare.

Rule 3. *Insure the Monkey:* Every monkey leaving your presence on the back of one of your people must be covered by one of two insurance policies:
    1. Recommend, Then Act
    2. Act, Then Advise

Rule 4. *Check on the Monkey:* Proper follow-up means healthier monkeys. Every monkey should have a checkup appointment.

So far, we have progressed from the disaster of my *working* all my people's monkeys to the point where I have *assigned* the monkeys to my staff. And you have learned how I applied the four rules of monkey management.

Let me now tell you about my progression to the ultimate degree of management, *delegation*, where my people are achieving more and more with less and less involvement from me. Assigning my staff's monkeys to them is miles ahead of working their monkeys myself, and delegation is light-years ahead of assigning. The best way to understand delegation (and how to achieve it) is to understand how it differs from assigning. Although many people use the words interchangeably, the words are, to quote Mark Twain, "as different as lightning from a lightning bug." That critical difference is one of the most valuable insights I gained from the "Managing Management Time" seminar:

*

*Assigning*
*Involves*
*A*
*Single*
*Monkey;*
*Delegation*
*Involves*
*A Family*
*Of Monkeys*

*

When I assigned a monkey to be handled by a member of my staff, I did most of the work of assigning. I asked my people to suggest "next moves" and then I either approved their suggestions or specified some "next moves" myself. Then I designated an owner for it, I insured it, and I scheduled and performed checkups on it. In other words, I assigned the monkeys, my people worked them.

We have since moved ahead to *delegation* where my staff are not only *working* their monkeys as before, they are also *assigning* them. Everything that was formerly done by them and me together, they are now doing on their own. In addition to working the monkeys, my people also identify them, insure them, assume ownership of them, and perform their own checkups on the monkeys. They themselves are applying Oncken's Rules of Monkey Management to their monkeys!

To put it differently, my people are now managing whole families of monkeys (projects) on their own for extended periods of time with minimal involvement from me. My involvement is limited to checking on the overall project from time to time, which means I don't have to get involved with the scores of individual monkeys that constitute the project, and a project checkup requires far less time than checking on each of the monkeys.

Between checkups my people are fully responsible for their projects (unless we encounter a problem that requires my intervention). As such, they are practicing *self-management*, which we all like a lot better than the high degree of *boss-management* they experienced when I was assigning monkeys to them.

In order to fully appreciate why delegation is the ultimate degree of professional management, let's recall a famous old definition of management: *Management is getting things done through others*. By that definition, the ultimate measure of management is *results*—the staff's output resulting from a manager's input. Other things being equal, the greater the ratio of output-to-input, the more effective the manager is.

Observe how the output-to-input ratio increased as I and my staff advanced from *doing* to *assigning* and then from *assigning* to *delegating*. When I was doing all the work myself, my output was equal to my input—one hour of input produced one hour of output. My department's output was sadly limited to the output of just one person . . . me!

Next, after some guidance from the One Minute Manager and learning from the seminar, I began assigning the monkeys to my people. My output-to-input ratio increased because every hour I spent assigning monkeys resulted in several hours of work produced by my staff. I welcomed that increase, but the ratio was still far too small because my input was still so large. (I was spending a lot of time on each individual monkey.) My department's output was still constrained by the large amount of time my people spent dealing with *me* and by the limited number of monkeys I had time to assign.

However, now that we have achieved the state of affairs called delegation, my output-to-input ratio has soared to many times what it was previously. My *input* is now dramatically lower— instead of doing all the work entailed in assigning scores of individual monkeys, I merely have to check on the condition of the whole project occasionally. And my department's *output* has now expanded enormously for two reasons: one, my people don't have to spend as much time with me as before, and two, they have more energy and motivation and morale for handling monkeys that are self-imposed than if the same monkeys were boss-imposed.

Moreover, reaching the state of delegation on one project frees up some time for me to pursue delegation on other projects. As I achieve delegation on more and more projects, more and more discretionary time is released to spend with my boss, peers, staff, and—myself.

Once delegation is reached, staying there is easy compared with the job of getting there. The state of "delegation" is analogous to an airplane at cruise altitude on automatic pilot where the pilot only monitors the flight and intervenes occasionally, if at all. But those interventions are minuscule in comparison with the energy and work the pilot expends in getting the plane away from the gate, down the runway, off the ground, and up to cruising altitude.

How does one attain this delightful state of delegation? The One Minute Manager explained that in its broadest sense, "coaching" is the term commonly used to signify the things managers do with their people to get projects up to "cruise altitude," where they can and will be handled mostly by staff members with minimal intervention by the manager. Remember:

*

*The
Purpose Of
Coaching
Is
To Get Into
Position
To
Delegate!*

*

What exactly has to happen before one is in position to delegate? Managers must not, indeed cannot, delegate until they are reasonably confident that (1) the project is on the right track, and (2) their people can successfully handle the project on their own. Managers who give their people full project responsibility and authority without such confidence are not delegating—they are abdicating responsibility.

Obviously, some projects can be delegated at the outset because it is sufficiently clear to the manager in the beginning how they should be handled and that staff members can successfully handle them.

However, most endeavors with the dimensions and complexities of a project cannot be delegated at the outset because often, in the beginning of a project, neither the manager nor his or her staff member has sufficient understanding of the problems, goals, options, timing, and ramifications to know even how to proceed, much less know whether that person can handle the project successfully. Thus, most projects require a period of coaching before the boss has sufficient confidence to enable him or her to delegate responsibly.

Obviously staff members *must* play a large role in building their boss's confidence to the point where the boss can delegate. In the first place, managers cannot delegate until their people have somehow demonstrated that they can handle the project.

Moreover, since people usually know more about their jobs than their bosses know, in many cases they should be persuading their bosses how the project should be handled. *This makes people just as responsible for coaching and delegation as their bosses are!*

The best way I know to explain the process of coaching is to describe a recent experience with one of my people, Gordon. As you will recall, he was my "monkey factory." This experience is one of my proudest accomplishments as a manager because I think it shows how much I and my people have improved in the past two years. First I will briefly describe what happened; then we can analyze it.

Some time ago it became apparent to me that one of our products might be having some technical problems in some of our customer locations. Before I got around to taking any action on the matter, Gordon, who was in charge of the product, stopped by my office one day and updated me on the situation. Only then did I realize that this had the potential of becoming a very costly and embarrassing problem. He had already prepared his recommendation for dealing with the problem so we made a date to meet the next day to discuss it.

Gordon conducted the meeting. His proposed solution consisted of a one-page synopsis followed by eighteen pages of supporting information in case it was needed. He read and then we discussed his synopsis, which contained a clear, brief description of the situation, three possible options for resolving it, the pros and cons of each option, and the option he recommended we adopt. As it turned out, no one was sure if the source of the problem was our company's product or the other products connected with it. So Gordon's solution included first a study to identify the nature and scope of the problem, and then corrective measures later if necessary to fix the problem.

It was soon obvious that Gordon had covered every detail of the technical part of the situation. (I was thankful he did, because my technical skills have necessarily diminished since I've been a manager.) He had determined what should be done, when, by whom, and how much it would cost. He specified all the resources he would need—budget, authority, and manpower—and the help he would need from me in arranging for them. His technical preparations left nothing to be desired.

However, there was a snag. Gordon had not fully considered how his proposed solution might be received by our sales people, the customers, and our higher management people. I explained that I was especially concerned about the reactions of two of our vice-presidents whose support would be critical to this endeavor, and I asked him what he thought we should do.

Gordon convinced me he could persuade the vice-presidents to support the project, so I asked him to meet with them to inform them of his plans and solicit their advice, and then report back to me before moving ahead on the project. When we met again he reported that despite his best efforts, one of the VPs still had serious reservations. He recommended that I speak to the VP. "Okay," I told Gordon, "I will do that, but you're going with me to watch what I do and help me as much as possible."

Two meetings with the VP and some minor changes to our plans resolved the problem and eliminated the last obstacle to my willingness to delegate the remainder of the project to Gordon, which I did. Then we made a date for a month afterward to go over the results of his study before we took any further steps. At that point, he took control of the project for a month, during which he handled dozens and dozens of monkeys on his own.

Now, let's analyze that scenario and look at the many things that helped me get into position to delegate—and let's pay special attention to *who* did those things!

1. *I cannot delegate until my anxieties allow it.* Gordon helped lower my anxieties by convincing me he could handle *most* aspects of the situation on his own. His thorough preparation and his skillful presentation plus his past record of success on similar projects were the main convincers. However, some residual anxieties caused me to retain control for a time. I maintained control by giving Gordon assignments (monkeys) which were insured at Level 1 (Recommend, Then Act). On assignments he could not handle alone, I worked the monkey *with* him—not *for* him—so I could do some teaching in the process.

2. *I can delegate only if I am reasonably sure my people know what is to be done.* But before they can know what to do, someone has to figure out what to do. If I figure it out, then I must tell them what to do (which is autocratic management). So Gordon figured out what to do himself, and then persuaded me he was right. That saved me a lot of time, and he was much more committed to his own ideas than any I might think up.

3. *It would be foolish to delegate to someone without reasonable assurance that he or she can get sufficient resources—time, information, money, people, assistance, and authority—to do the work.* But who could know better than Gordon what resources he needed? That's why *he* took the initiative to determine what these resources were. Moreover, on his own Gordon arranged for as many of the resources as possible, asking for my help in arranging only those things he could not get for himself.

4. *I cannot turn control of any project over to anyone until I am confident that the cost and timing and quantity and quality of the project will be acceptable.* To leave those items open-ended would be abdicating my responsibility as a manager. But in order to *agree* on standards of performance, we must first *have* some, which means that someone must produce them. The person who should produce them is the person who is in the best position to know what the standards should be. Gordon was, he did, and he convinced me to approve them.

5. It is clear that the more committed my people are to their projects the greater the odds of their projects' success. Other things being equal, *the more commitment my people show, the more comfortable I will be in delegating to them.* Gordon took care of his own commitment. The time and effort he *invested* in his proposal increased his commitment. The fact that it was *his* proposal increased his commitment, as did his personal pride in doing a job well. Gordon's implicit promise to me to do the work sealed his commitment. Because his commitment was internally generated, I did not have to resort to requests or contracts or coercion to gain his commitment.

This is not an exhaustive list of things that have to happen before delegation can occur, but it illustrates the process. Regarding Gordon, I'm sure you noticed that I maintained control of the project until I was confident I could delegate control to him. But *he* initiated and carried out most of the "next moves" that got us to the point of delegation. That was as it should be. Since the purpose of coaching is to get my people to the point where they can succeed on their own, it would defeat the purpose if I were to do anything, even in the coaching process, that they could do themselves.

The coaching process usually consists of staff members carrying out a series of assignments while managers control and direct the process until they are confident their people can assume control for an extended period on their own. As the assignments are carried out, both the manager and his or her people gain time and information they can use to sharpen their thinking about where the project should be heading. As they both become more confident that the project is on the right track and as the boss's confidence in the person's competence grows, the boss gradually delegates more and more project responsibility. The assignments should be boss-initiated *only to the extent the staff member cannot initiate them*. Usually, the first assignments are for the subordinate to develop and propose a "game plan." If necessary, the boss redirects the plan until it is acceptable to him or her. Then, if the parties are still not in position to delegate, the next assignments are for the subordinate to make some "next moves" on the project itself with the boss guiding and controlling the process until delegation can occur. You can see from this that, usually, delegation is not just an act; it is usually a state of affairs that exists only after sufficient coaching enables the boss to delegate responsibly.

Of course, not all coaching experiences are as easy as the one just described. But they tend to get easier after managers and their people go through the process a few times because everyone learns to anticipate and complement the other, much like a passer and receiver on a football team. After sufficient practice a quarterback can throw the ball to a spot on the field before the receiver ever turns toward that spot because he knows exactly where the receiver will be going and exactly when he will arrive. Furthermore, each can make the other a better player. With a great catch the receiver can make a poor pass successful, and with a great pass the thrower can make the receiver successful. Likewise with managers and their people. Once they learn to work together they can achieve the point where people conceive and implement most of their work, while the boss merely ratifies what is being done.

A lot has happened since the One Minute Manager told me about Oncken's monkey management. When I think how much my life has changed, I sometimes recall the story of the man who, when asked how long he had been working for his company, replied, "Ever since they threatened to fire me!"

Like him, I was shocked into action. The conversion wasn't always easy. I encountered a good deal of resistance and I made some mistakes. But I finally got the responsibility where it should be, and things have never been the same since, and they never will be the same again!

As I applied the concepts I've learned, my people became more self-managed than ever before. That made them feel better and perform better. They became more self-reliant, which gave me more time to manage other relationships that were vital to my department's success.

Let me pause here for a moment or two and reflect on those other relationships and one last important lesson I got from the Oncken "Managing Management Time" seminar. While monkey management is key to controlling what Oncken called "subordinate-imposed" time (where a boss is handling monkeys that his or her people should be caring for and feeding), success in management requires that we constantly strike a proper balance among three categories of time:

# *THREE KINDS OF ORGANIZATIONAL TIME:*

### BOSS-IMPOSED TIME

### SYSTEM-IMPOSED TIME

### SELF-IMPOSED TIME

BOSS-*imposed time* is time you and I spend doing things we would not be doing if we did not have bosses. No one has to have a boss; one can retire, go on welfare, win the lottery, or become an entrepreneur, and thereby avoid having one. But having a boss *requires* some of our time because of the Golden Rule of Management: THOSE WHO HAVE THE GOLD MAKE THE RULES!

Because bosses have Golden Rule clout, we intuitively understand that it's to our advantage that they be satisfied with our work. Keeping bosses satisfied takes time, but dealing with dissatisfied ones takes even more time.

For example, back in the days when I was so busy with my staff's monkeys, one of my many mistakes was not taking time to keep my boss well-enough informed about what was going on. As a result, she got an embarrassing surprise one day when her boss uncovered a big problem I should have warned her about in advance.

Her reaction was to institute a whole new set of reports from me to her. That took more of my time than if I had kept her informed in the first place.

How do I keep my boss satisfied with my work? Here is the best expression on how to do it I've ever heard. Always do what your boss wants. If you don't like what your boss wants, *change what your boss wants*, but always do what your boss wants.

This is not to say that we should always agree with our bosses. On the contrary:

*

*If
You Always
Agree
With
Your Boss,
One
Of You
Is Not
Necessary*

*

But it is to your advantage to satisfy your boss. So if you disagree with what your boss wants, treat your boss the same way you want your people to treat you when they disagree with something you want. We call it *loyal opposition*. That's when you try to convince your boss to accept some better alternative; but failing that, always wholeheartedly do what he or she wants.

One of the most important lessons of my career is that good work alone, no matter how much it satisfies *you*, might not be enough to satisfy your boss. Satisfying your boss takes time, sometimes over and above the time it takes to do the good work. I realize it takes time to keep *my* boss informed, to protect her from embarrassing surprises, to anticipate how she wants things handled, to build a record of success so she feels more comfortable giving me more autonomy, and so on.

We neglect doing these things at our peril. Believe me, I know from experience that failing to invest sufficient time to satisfy my boss will soon result in more and more boss-imposed time, which, of course, means less and less time available to spend with my peers or associates and staff and on the things I would like to do.

SYSTEM-*imposed time* is time we spend on the administrative and related demands from people (peers/associates) other than our bosses and our own staffs, demands that are part of every organization. This is the time spent as just one of a seemingly countless number of pulleys on an endless administrative conveyor belt crisscrossing the organizational chart, dropping things off and picking things up. For you, the drop-off point is your "in basket" and the pick-up point is your "out basket." System-imposed time includes administrative forms to be completed, meetings you have to attend, and phone calls you must handle.

For example, if your secretary elopes, that creates in your department what is called in Personnel language "an unfilled vacancy." (When they fill it they call it a "filled vacancy.") If you ask them to hire another secretary for you, they will ask you to fill out a form, write a job description, and so on. The time you spend dealing with these matters is system-imposed time. Some people call it red tape, some call it administrivia, some call it bureaucracy.

Administrative red tape exists in virtually all organizations because staff departments that employ people to support everyone in line management are typically overworked and understaffed.

A support person once explained to me why things are this way: "There is no limit to how much can be asked of us, but there is definitely a limit to how much we can do!" Therefore, support people can't possibly do everything that is requested of them. So, in order to bring order out of chaos and to make their own lives a little easier, they develop wondrous varieties of forms, policies, procedures, and manuals.

The red tape takes time, so a lot of people complain about it. But ignoring the system's requirements is risky. Oncken told a wonderful story about a manager whose chair had collapsed and who wanted it replaced. Because he was busy he had not taken the time to get to know anyone in Purchasing, nor did he take the time to go see them face to face to request a new chair. Instead, he made his request over the phone.

He was under a lot of pressure at the time and was annoyed because of the broken chair so he was somewhat curt to the person in Purchasing. The equally curt reply was "We'll have to have that request in writing. And on the proper form." He didn't have the proper form so he walked over to Purchasing and, trying to keep his cool but obviously annoyed, filled out the form right there and shoved it across the desk.

Ten days later (when he was expecting his new chair) that request form showed up in his in basket with a note stapled to it that said, "Sorry. We cannot process this request because you have the wrong authorization number in Box 9." He was livid. He called Purchasing and chewed them out. When he finally calmed down he asked them, "What is the right number?" With an audible chuckle the clerk gave him an answer that was quick and to the point: "Let's get something straight. Our job is to spot the wrong numbers and your job is to fill in the right ones." The manager repaired the old chair himself.

We can't manage without the support of these people, and we need them more than they need us. So, in order to survive within the organization, we have to conform to the red-tape requirements of the system. If we give their requirements short shrift in order to spend our time elsewhere, they can penalize us in ways that require even more system-imposed time.

THE third kind of time we must manage successfully is *self-imposed time*, which is time spent doing the things *we* decide to do, not things done strictly in response to the initiatives of our bosses, peers, and the people who report to us. You can't be a self-starter without self-imposed time.

Self-imposed time is the most important of the three types of time because that's the only time in which we have discretion to express our own individuality within an organization. In boss-imposed time the boss's requirements take precedence over our own individuality. In system-imposed time the need to conform takes precedence. Therefore, it is only with self-imposed time that we make our own unique contribution to an organization.

Self-imposed time, like cholesterol, comes in two varieties, good and bad: discretionary and subordinate-imposed. Subordinate-imposed time, as we have explained, is time spent working on your staff's monkeys. (It is obviously self-imposed because we can elect whether to pick up the monkeys or not.)

DISCRETIONARY time is time in which we do the things that make our work truly rewarding over and above financial compensation—things such as creating, innovating, leading, planning, and organizing. And these activities are needed in organizations for growth and progress and to remain viable and competitive. Discretionary time is thus vital to individuals and to the organization.

Although discretionary time is the most vital time of all, it is, unfortunately, the first to disappear when the pressure is on, as I learned so well in the school of hard knocks.

Why? The reason has to do with the incentive system. You see, if we don't comply with our bosses' wishes we will be guilty of *insubordination*. If we don't conform to the system's requirements we will be guilty of *noncooperation*. If we don't do what we promised for our staff, that is, work off their monkeys, we will be guilty of *procrastination*. We are very reluctant to be guilty of such organizational sins because:

*Swift And Obvious
Penalties
Pursue Those
Who Treat Other People's
Requirements In A
Lighthearted,
Cavalier Fashion!*

*

But, what is the penalty for neglecting the most important kind of time of all: discretionary time? For instance, what is the penalty for neglecting to do the things I dream up in my discretionary time (especially if no one else knows about them)? There is no penalty, at least in the short term, because nobody can accuse me of not doing what they never knew I intended to do in the first place.

So discretionary activities (which carry no immediate penalties) compete for my time with activities which, if neglected, make me guilty of either insubordination, noncooperation, or procrastination. Guess which ones take precedence!

While neglecting discretionary time might be safe in the short run, in the long run the penalties are severe both to the organization and to myself. The long-term penalty to the organization is that it cannot survive, much less progress, without the benefits that flow *only* from the discretionary time of its employees; that is, if employees have no discretionary time, the organization will be denied their creativity, innovation, initiative, et cetera. The long-term penalty to me is that organizational life becomes a living death in which all I do is react to problems created by others, and I never have time to create and innovate and initiate on my own.

WHAT to do, then? Given the ongoing requirement of constantly maintaining the interconnected relationships among my boss, peers, and staff, how did I extricate myself from the mess I was in two years ago?

Although it is imperative that we manage all three relationships concurrently, we have to *start* somewhere. I started by eliminating subordinate-imposed time. There are two reasons for starting this way. One reason is that subordinate-imposed time does not belong in my schedule. The second is that some drastic changes had to be made quickly, and making such changes can make other people nervous. I didn't want to make anybody nervous, but if I had to do so, prudence dictated that they be the people with the least power to retaliate. Subordinates cannot impose extra monkeys on me without my cooperation, but bosses and peers can and will do so if I ignore their requirements in order to acquire some time to get my recovery jump-started.

So I began by eliminating subordinate-imposed time. That gave me an equal amount of discretionary time (since self-imposed time is the sum of discretionary time plus subordinate-imposed time), which I used to begin my managerial recovery process.

AT the "Managing Management Time" seminar I heard an interesting story to illustrate the process. It's the story of two fellows running side by side through the woods, being chased by a bear. The bear was gaining. One fellow said to the other, "If I had my running shoes I could run a little faster." The other fellow replied, "I still don't think you could outrun the bear," to which came the retort, "I don't have to outrun the bear. I just have to outrun you!"

I found that even though you get a step ahead, the bear is still there! In my case, eliminating subordinate-imposed time gave me that extra step, but other demands on my time still existed, panting close behind: demands from my boss and peers, and legitimate requests from my staff. But the newly gained discretionary time gave me some room to get a handle on those other demands.

Once I got that little seed of discretionary time, I planted it carefully and made it grow. First, with my boss, I took time to figure out how to do my work in a way to build her confidence to the point where she began allowing me more and more discretion.

For example, there are many areas of my work where I previously could take no action until I checked with her first; she wanted to know my plans in advance so she could have a chance to forestall mistakes I might make.

All that checking with her took a lot of time for both of us. Since then, however, my record of success in those same areas has lowered her anxieties to the point where I am allowed to handle them on my own and inform her of what I did afterward in my quarterly report. This saves both of us a lot of time. In other words, I used my newly gained discretionary time in a way that gave me (and her!) even more discretionary time.

I followed a similar approach with my peers. In the past I had been relying solely on the authority of my position to get things done because I was too busy to deal with situations in more productive ways. And I paid for it. But once I got some discretionary time, I spent some of it building my relationships with people in the system and I found that the more rapport we had the more they would do for me with less effort on my part.

Again, just a short example will illustrate the process. In the past, if I urgently needed something from a staff person, the best I could get was routine, by-the-book effort ("Fill out the form and we'll go to work on it").

But in recent months I have invested some discretionary time in building better relationships with them. Now when I need something urgently I get their wholehearted support and it takes less of my time to get it—this from the very same system I used to criticize as bureaucratic, unwieldy, and unresponsive. Again, as with my boss, I have invested discretionary time to create even more discretionary time. In my dealings with the system I have learned that however inept it may be, the people who operate it can make it do wonders for me if they will. So rather than criticizing and resenting the imperfect system, I practice this philosophy: *It is better to strike a straight blow with a crooked stick than spend my whole life trying to straighten the darn thing out.*

Likewise with my people. As you now all too well know, in the space of a single morning (that "famous" Monday morning) I returned their monkeys to them and, in the process, converted several days of subordinate-imposed time into an equal amount of discretionary time. Then I began coaching my people along toward greater self-reliance. Every incremental increase in their self-reliance meant an equivalent increase in my discretionary time and in their morale. (There is a high correlation between self-reliance and morale.)

I now clearly measure my success by what I am able to get my people to do, not what I do myself. Fortunately, my boss measures me that way as well. And I am happy to report that I will soon be taking over a larger area of responsibility. I feel great, and I've been told I even look better than ever. Although I'm still busy, I no longer feel the pressed-for-time anxiety that I once did. The physical and emotional distress that were my constant companions before I learned monkey management are now just bad memories.

This all came about because I have learned to think differently about my work. My mentality has changed from that of a *do-er* to that of a *manager*. As such, I have not only learned the practice of monkey management, but also I have learned to replace the psychological rewards of *doing* with the rewards of *managing*, namely, deriving satisfaction from what my people do and being recognized, paid, and promoted accordingly.

What encouraged me most was seeing how my people responded to my new management style and how much their productivity and morale improved. Their performance enabled me to build a high degree of confidence in them, which meant that in many cases my involvement in a project amounted to little more than ratifying what they were doing.

The improved relationship with my staff was the first step in reversing the *vicious* cycle I was in and creating a *vital* cycle which, like the vicious one, is enormously powerful and feeds on itself. As my people responded to my improved management style, their productivity and morale improved, causing me to be less anxious about their work and allowing me to give them more freedom, thus releasing my time to invest elsewhere. I invested some of my newly found time with my boss, causing her anxieties to diminish and allowing her to give me more freedom. I also invested some time in improving my relationships with the people in the "system" to the point where I got more done in less time. I especially had time to better manage our customer and supplier relationships that are so key to our long-term survival.

Finally, one day, the vital cycle gave me a small surplus of that rare and precious commodity— discretionary time. I used that surplus time to begin pursuing (for the first time in a long time) some of the discretionary activities on my own agenda that make managerial life worthwhile. In other words, I began to do some manag*ing* instead of just being manag*ed*.

IN the past, I spent much of my time fighting fires; now I can prevent most of the fires by spending just a little time in advance. In the past, I spent a great deal of my time reacting to other people; now I spend a great deal of my time in proactive measures. These include doing some advance planning for a change so we can do the right things the right way the first time instead of having to do them over so often.

I came to realize that when people throughout the organization have responsibility for managing their own monkeys, it's hard to tell who's a worker and who's a manager because everyone is committed to doing what it takes to do the best job possible.

Besides the changes in my own personal and professional life, I have begun to share my learnings with others I know—especially those time-pressed individuals who never seem to have enough time for their work, family, or friends. I help them to see the dynamics of monkey management and to become monkey managers in the zoo of their choice. This new way of life has changed my life and the lives of those around me.

Finally, perhaps the greatest lesson I have learned about monkey management, at work and at home, is that there are always more monkeys clamoring for attention than we have time to manage. Unless we are extremely careful which ones we accept responsibility for, it is very easy to wind up caring for the wrong monkeys while the really important ones are starving for lack of attention. If we thoughtlessly try to handle all of them, our efforts will be diluted to the point where none of them are healthy.

I hope this monkey tale will help you as much as it has helped me, which is enormously. I am constantly reminded of its benefits. For example, as I write these final words, I am alone in my office. My door is open. And as I glance at the new photograph of my family, I notice one major change: I'M NOW IN THE PICTURE!

The
End

The
Beginning
Share It with Others!

# 01 *Praisings*

We would like to give a public praising to a number of important people who played key roles in making this book a reality:

*Robert Nelson*, a very talented writer and vice-president of product development for Blanchard Training and Development, Inc. (BTD), for his assistance with the writing, editing, and coordination of this book.

*Eleanor Terndrup*, secretary extraordinaire, for her tireless effort in typing numerous drafts of this book over a four-year period.

*William Oncken III* and *Ramona Neel* of the William Oncken Corporation, for their invaluable assistance in editing the manuscript and helping to keep the content consistent with the "Managing Management Time" seminar.

*George Heaton* of Blanchard Training and Development, Canada, for providing the original spark from which this project grew.

*Margret McBride* for being our literary agent and providing constant support.

All the folks at William Morrow and Company, Inc., particularly *Larry Hughes*, *Al Marchioni*, our editor *Pat Golbitz*, and her assistant, *Jill Hamilton*, for continuing to believe in *The One Minute Manager Library* and supporting this addition to it.

*Jim Ballard* for his creative energy around "Rescuers Anonymous," and *Stephen Karpman*, for defining the term "rescuer" for us.

*Paul Hersey* for teaching us some of the lessons from Little League.

*Marjorie Blanchard*, *Margaret Oncken*, and *Alice Burrows* for their constant love and support throughout the peaks and valleys of our lives.

# ⓪¹ *About the Authors*

**Kenneth Blanchard,** co-developer of the One Minute Manager and Situational Leadership, is an internationally known author, educator, consultant/ trainer, and professor of leadership and organization behavior at the University of Massachusetts, Amherst. He has written extensively in the fields of leadership, motivation, and managing change, including the ground-breaking *One Minute Manager Library* series, co-authored with some of the top management thinkers in the country, *The Power of Ethical Management,* co-authored with Dr. Norman Vincent Peale, and the widely used and acclaimed Prentice-Hall text *Management of Organizational Behavior,* co-authored with Paul Hersey, now in its fifth edition.

Dr. Blanchard received his B.A. in government and philosophy from Cornell University, an M.A. in sociology and counseling from Colgate University, and a Ph.D. in educational administration and management from Cornell University, where he presently serves on the Board of Trustees.

As chairman of the board of Blanchard Training and Development, Inc., a San Diego-based human-resource-development company he co-founded with his wife, Marjorie, Dr. Blanchard has trained over two hundred thousand managers and his approaches to management have been incorporated into many *Fortune 500* companies as well as numerous fast-growing entrepreneurial companies.

***William Oncken, Jr.,*** was one of the most articulate spokesmen in the field of management. After his graduation from Princeton in 1934, Bill learned from practical experience that a manager's ability to generate and profitably use discretionary time is crucial to his career competitiveness and to his organization's ability to survive and prosper in our free-enterprise system. He translated his observations and practical experience into his internationally known MANAGING MANAGEMENT TIME and MANAGING MANAGERIAL INITIATIVE seminars; his revolutionary article "Managing Management Time: Who's Got the Monkey?" (co-authored with Donald Wass); and his recently published book, *Managing Management Time*, destined to become a classic of management literature.

Mr. Oncken founded his own company in 1960. Based in Dallas, The William Oncken Corporation continues to provide his high-quality management development programs, teaching his unique managerial philosophy and perspective.

For more than three decades the fruits of his creative genius, his MANAGING MANAGEMENT TIME seminar, has helped managers generate and fully utilize that most precious managerial commodity: discretionary time.

*The One Minute Manager Meets the Monkey* is adapted from and emphasizes the "staff" strategy of "Oncken's Management Molecule."

When it comes to management time *Hal Burrows* speaks with authority. His experience at two *Fortune 500* companies and fifteen years of running his own consulting firm as well as his ability to communicate his insights with wit and flair have made him a very popular speaker on the subject of management and negotiating. Since 1973 his face-to-face experience with thousands of managers at all levels from hundreds of private companies and government agencies has enabled him to help them become more successful in their careers. In addition to speaking at conventions and other major meetings, Burrows presents two highly acclaimed seminars: Managing Management Time, and Managing Negotiations Under Pressure.

Hal is also a successful entrepreneur in the area of commercial real estate development in Raleigh, North Carolina (P.O. Box 52070, Raleigh, NC 27612, 919-787-9769), where he and his family reside.

## Find Out More

In 1979 Ken Blanchard founded The Ken Blanchard Companies to support organisations looking to put the principles of his books into practice. Now a major international management consultancy and training organisation, the company works with many of the world's leading businesses to unleash the full power and potential of their people. The Ken Blanchard Companies is perhaps best known as the originator of the most widely used leadership development process, Situational Leadership® II and also specialises in Team Building, Organisational Change and Customer Service. Consultancy services, in-house training, public workshops, coaching, speakers and a wide variety of learning materials are also provided through a network of offices in 30 countries worldwide. If *The One Minute Manager Meets the Monkey* has inspired you to transform your business, contact:

The Ken Blanchard Companies
Gateway Guildford
Power Close
Guildford
Surrey
GU1 1FJ
Tel: + 44 (0) 1483 456000
Email: uk@kenblanchard.com
Website: www.kenblanchard.com

# RAVING FANS!

A Revolutionary Approach to Customer Service

## Ken Blanchard and Sheldon Bowles

'Your customers are only satisfied because their expectations are so low and because no one else is doing better ... If you really want a booming business, you have to create Raving Fans.'

Written in the parable style of the bestselling *The One Minute Manager*, it uses a brilliantly simple and charming story to teach how to define a vision, learn what a customer really wants, institute effective systems and make Raving Fan Service a constant feature, not just a passing fad.

By the authors of *Gung Ho!*, *Big Bucks!* and *High Five!*, *Raving Fans!* includes startling new tips and innovative techniques that can help anyone in any workplace to deliver stunning customer service and achieve miraculous bottom-line results.

# GUNG HO!

How to Motivate People In Any Organisation

## Ken Blanchard and Sheldon Bowles

Increase productivity, profits and your own prosperity! Every day, thousands of uninspired employees trudge to work, often dooming their companies to failure with their lack of motivation.

*Gung Ho!* outlines foolproof ways to increase productivity by fostering excellent morale in the workplace. Drawing on over 20 years' experience of working with hundreds of corporations, Ken Blanchard and Sheldon Bowles reveal a sure-fire system for boosting employee enthusiasm, energy and performance.

By the authors of *Raving Fans!*, *Big Bucks!* and *High Five!*, and written in the style of the world-beating *One Minute Manager* series, *Gung Ho!* is based on three core ideas to ensure that employees are committed to success and presents a clear game-plan for implementing them.

# BIG BUCKS!

## Make Serious Money For You and Your Company

### Ken Blanchard and Sheldon Bowles

*Big Bucks!* offers new and irresistible practical advice to create money and get rich. Like *The One Minute Manager* and *Raving Fans!*, this book uses a business parable to demonstrate how to overcome three challenges – the Test of Joy, the Test of Purpose and the Test of Creativity – to achieve spectacular financial success.

Through a series of easy-to-follow steps and powerful strategies, Blanchard and Bowles show how you can gain wealth and create lasting prosperity. They reveal how, by focusing on concepts like commitment, intensity, purpose and even fun, anyone can build personal wealth and financial security.

Best of all, *Big Bucks!* shows how to accomplish even more valuable achievements by being generous with your time, talents and prosperity, giving significance and meaning to your millions.

# THE ON-TIME, ON-TARGET MANAGER

How a 'Last-Minute Manager'
Conquered Procrastination

## Ken Blanchard and Steve Gottry

In every workplace, in every industry, there lurks a diabolical career killer – procrastination. *The On-Time, On-Target Manager* tells the highly recognizable story of Bob, a typical middle manager who tends to put things off to the last minute. As a result, he misses deadlines because his lack of focus causes him to accomplish all the meaningless tasks before he can get to the important things.

Luckily, Bob is sent to his company's 'Chief Effectiveness Officer' who helps him deal with the three negative side effects of procrastination: lateness, poor work quality and stress. Bob learns how to overcome procrastination, transforming himself from a crisis-prone Last-Minute manager into a productive On-Time, On-Target manager.

With this engaging parable, Ken Blanchard and Steve Gottry tackle the problem of procrastination head-on, offering practical strategies any professional can immediately put into practice to improve performance.